# wheels

# Bob Graham

Blackie

This is Tom.
He is looking for a place to ride his new tricycle.

He tries the grass.
No, that won't do!
The wheels sink in.
Try somewhere else, Tom.

Tom tries a puddle.
He makes a splash.
It's lots of fun.

Tom tries some mud.
Now his wheels sink in so far
that he can't move at all.

Tom wonders if Terry the Terror can help.

No! That is no use.
The tricycle won't move if the
front wheel is not on the ground.

He tries the carpet.
That is no better than the grass.
The wheels sink in here too.

It's much easier to push the pedals
on the kitchen floor.
Watch out Terry!

Mum says, "Don't play in the kitchen!"

Tom looks for a place that is hard
and smooth like the kitchen floor.

Look at him go!

The wheels do not sink into the hard garden path.

The path is better than the grass
and the puddles…

...and better than the mud and the carpet.

Tom has found the best place to ride his new tricycle.
Now can he stop?